CAT TALES

I0555158

By Wayne McDonald
Illustrated by BJ McDonald

Praise for Cat's Tales

"This book is a delightful and humorous reminder of how quirky cats are by nature, and how fun it can be to imagine life through their eyes. Cattitude to the max! There are so many excellent choices for my favorite tale that I'm happy to imagine myself with nine lives to read them all over again."
- Andy S. Centennial, CO

"My wife, kids and I are all cat lovers. We loved reading the well written prose and background stories associated with these amazing creatures.   The illustrations are superb, and the author paints vivid pictures of the nuances and eccentricities of the feline world. We highly recommend this adventure into the fun and funny world of cats!!"
- The Millers

Copyright 2025

Paperback ISBN: 978-1-953686-45-9
Hardcover ISBN: 978-1-953686-46-6
Library of Congress Control Number: 2025944118

All rights reserved including the right of reproduction in whole or in part in any form without written permission from the publisher. Copies of the illustrations may be obtained through the illustrator's website.

Living Springs
Publishers

WWW.LivingSpringsPublishers.com
Centennial, CO

Acknowledgement

I wish to thank the following for helping me write my book about the domestic house cat.

Marj McDonald, who has put up with my little poems for over 40 years.

BJ McDonald, my daughter/illustrator who makes my books so much better.

Jordan McDonald, my son who helps me with business and tech questions, and who also designed my website.

Kelsey Reynolds, the Arapahoe County librarian who continues to support me and provide great guidance.

Wonderful public-school librarians (Kim Caster, Camille Clark, and Mary Beth Cline) who have assisted me in so many ways.

Gudy Gaskill Elementary School staff and students, who have provided feedback to help me improve my poems.

Table of Contents

This Book
Is
Dedicated
To

Cat

Lovers

Everywhere!

OTHER BOOKS BY WAYNE MCDONALD

Can You Guess Who I Am? (Book 1)

Can You Guess Who I Am? (Book 2)

About This Book
My first two books contained animal riddle
rhymes, while this book is entirely different.
It contains short poems about domestic
house cats that lived or are living today.
The poems are based on the information
I found while researching kitty cats.

CASPER

Casper of Plymouth, England, each day
A public bus rode 11 miles both ways
Brits thought it was neat
He'd take the same seat
But the bus fee he never did pay!

This black and white cat – tis true
Was adopted from a shelter in 2002
From home he'd escape
Thought exploring was great
Toured offices and napped there, too

At the day's end, he knew it was time
And got on the bus on the No. 3 line
From there he rode
Back to his abode
Made it home for dinner just fine

He became famous at home, you see
And was seen on the BBC
Book about him was written
The British were smitten
As they read about Casper with glee!

NOTE: The author Susan Finden wrote
the book about Casper and titled it
Casper the Commuting Cat.

Casper reportedly once visited
a doctor's office, found a seat,
and took a nap. Now that's a
"cheeky" fellow!

(**Cheeky** can mean arrogant or shameless.)

THE DOMESTIC HOUSE CAT

Scientists tell us
And this info is new
We're 95% tiger
And 90% like you

We learn short words
The words are your choice
And we tie the word
To the sound of your voice

We lick ourselves clean
While you need those showers
We sleep more than wake
While you sleep 8 hours

We lick a bone clean
With a tongue that's so rough
While you need a knife
To cut the tough stuff

We are great hunters
We do slink around
And while we are hunting
We don't make a sound

CRÈME PUFF

Crème puff, longest lived cat, they say
Was blessed with **38** years and **3** days
In Texas did live
Where owner did give
Her broccoli and eggs – a mainstay

She also dined on coffee with cream
Not a cat's diet that I've ever seen!
While cooling her "toes"
Watched nature shows
In the garage on a nice TV screen

Her owner, a plumber named Jake
Thought every feline was great
He adopted a lot
Housed'm at his home spot
Rehomed them, improving their lot

Jake adopted hundreds of them
'Cause he loved'm, not on a whim
Was it the food he did give
That long helped them live
Or the love he showed all of them?

NOTE: The Guinness Book of World
Records declared Crème Puff the
oldest domestic house cat to
have ever lived. Crème Puff
finally departed for cat heaven
on August 6, 2005.

CAT EYES

You see colors, so many you do
Red, orange, green, yellow, and blue
But a house cat does not see all that
It sees fewer colors than you

To the cat, blue and yellow are seen
But reds and pinks just look green
What's purple to you, cat sees as blue
But do not your house cat demean!

At depth perception, it does so excel
This helps it hunt prey so very well
Sees well in low light, gives prey fright
So for hunting, cat eyes are swell

If you wanna buy your cat a toy
One – that it – will surely enjoy
Buy one in blue or yellow, too
You'll fill its cat life with joy!

DUSTY
THE "KLEPTO" KITTY

For thievery, **Dusty** stands tall
"Slickied" anything he could haul
Sneaked off with so much
That with the use of a truck
Could've restocked stores at the mall

This Siamese took what he pleased
Prowlin' at night, sneakin' 'tween trees
From rubber toys to car wash mitts
From bathing suits to a blanket
Quickly did see, seize, and flee

"Kleptomaniac" defines this dude
Stole without care, seems sorta rude
This recurrent urge
He just could not purge
And on nearby backyards did intrude

Now, amidst all the plunder
His owners did wonder
If related was he
To Butch "Cat-sidy"
As fences he climbed o'er and under

NOTE: Dusty lived in San Mateo, CA.
Adopted from the Humane Society,
his "cat burglar" career began when
he was two. The list of items he
stole also included dish towels,
wash clothes, towels, shoes,
underwear, balls, leg warmers,
Frisbees, a golf club head cover,
pajama pants, etc. His notoriety
expanded when Animal Planet
aired a profile on him in 2011. We
will never know what led to his
"life of crime."

MORE ABOUT THE KITTY CAT

With body language and
With sounds so many
We talk to you people
And we tell you plenty

We have 18 toes
And paws, we have 4
And like the cougar
We purr but don't roar

Sometimes we critters
Must deal with some falls
From 3 to 10 feet
We land on our paws

But when we climb trees
Get high off the ground
We might need a human
To bring us back down

MAX

In Randolph Center, Vermont
On a beautiful campus spot
Sat a cat named **Max**
Totally relaxed
'Cause he knew he'd won the jackpot

Obtained his doctorate, you see
From Vermont State U. for free
His studies, for sure
Were in "Litter-ature"
For a cat tis the "purr-fect" degree

All day on campus does roam
Then when it's time to go home
A student may collect him
They'd never neglect him
Love him like a dog loves a bone

13

This tri-colored cat just has it made
Hanging with students in the tree shade
In the Green Mountain State
Where one can't debate
This cat has now made the grade!

NOTE: What a life! A stress reducing, emotional support cat, who came by the role accidentally, walks to "work" and gives and receives love every day. Then, around 5 p.m., if he is still at school, might just get a ride back home, sometimes in a student's backpack. Check him out online at *Vermont State University, Randolph Center, Vermont.*

CATTITUDE

I'm 4,000 years less domesticated than
That dog you call "man's best friend"
So cut me some slack, get off my back!
I'm doing the best that I can

My "cattitude" is not like your mutt
I'm more independent and I do strut
My stuff in your house
And might catch a mouse
Might want your attention BUT

At times don't care for petting, you see
I know I'm superior, that's just me
I'm self-assured; cannot be cured
Of thinking I "lord over thee"

Wanna pet that knows it's in charge?
Wanna pet that really lives large?
Then get thee a cat
'Cause we're where it's at
I'll be the colonel, you'll be the sarge
TEN-HUT!

MAYOR STUBBS

Way up there in Alaska so cold
They elected a kitty mayor, I'm told
Stubbs was his name
And he came to fame
Here the story for you I'll unfold

This orange tabby with a stubby tail
Up in Talkeetna it did dwell
Few wanted to run
For mayor, so for fun
They "elected" a cat. Do tell!

For 20 years he served the town
Getting free meals, roaming around
But things looked dire
When he fell in a fryer
But with good care he did rebound

Go visit Talkeetna in summertime
Go to Nagley's store when the sun shines
And there you will see
Roaming happy and free
His successor, Aurora, so fine

NOTE: Stubbs was found as a kitten and taken to live in Nagley's General Store. Some locals took a vote and jokingly elected Stubbs mayor. As the mayor for 20 years, he would roam around town to get fed by residents. In the afternoon, he would drink a catnip and water mixture, served in a wine glass, at a nearby restaurant. Mayor Stubbs was succeeded by Mayor Denali, who was then replaced by his sister, Mayor Aurora.

THE TAIL TELL EVIDENCE

Heads up, you humans! I'm here to teach
Learning you need that's within your reach
Don't get in detention, no, just pay attention
And you'll pass this class in cat speech

I'm not a dog and I do not drool
Surely you learned that already in school
I can leap high and dogs I **decry***
And in my own way I do rule

If against you I'm rubbing, tail standing tall
I'm happy as a kid with friends at the mall
If these signs you see, well, you can pet me
Then feed me and I'll be **enthralled****

If I head bump you, tis a good sign
We get along, I like you just fine
And if I slow blink, well, "whaddaya" think?
Means you're my human, I think you're
MINE!

*DECRY: LOOK DOWN ON.   **ENTHRALLED: DELIGHTED

MISS MISADVENTURE

A tabby named **Bynx** climbed a tree so high
Higher and higher up toward the sky
Up to 185 feet
Got scared and just could not retreat

In Washington State, where trees grow great
Bynx did climb higher and tempted fate
Canopy Cat Rescue got the call
And Mr. Tom Otto prevented a fall

Tom spoke "cat" to calm **Bynx** down
And got her safely back to the ground
When cats climb high and lose their "calm"
They need rescuers just like Tom

So many cats – Tom has rescued
For when scared owners on him intrude
Tom gives it his best, has to be shrewd
To keep kitties from coming "unglued"

NOTE: Squirrels can rotate their rear ankles and feet to climb down a tree face first. You have probably seen them do this. Cats can easily climb up a tree but do not come with this "rotating" ability, and most never graduate from "climbing down backwards" school. Hence, the problem. Cat owners are very thankful for people like Tom.

WATCH OUT!

If my tail is lowered, rapidly swishing
I'm agitated, so don't go a-wishing
To pet me right now
For you'll see me scowl
And sharp claws you'll find I'm a-dishing

If there's puffed up fur on body and tail
Don't pet me now, won't turn out so well
If I'm growling or hissing
You shouldn't be missing
My "talk" or I'll scratch and you'll wail

These are a few of the signs I send
So pay attention and we'll still be friends
Yes, chilled I can be
But moods change, you see
I'm just a kitty, don't mean to offend

ORANGEY THE CAT ACTOR

This orange, domestic short-haired tabby
Did have a personality crabby
Not a team player
Was a project delayer
Who used his sharp claws go grabby

Yes, he was famous for acting for years
But scratched, bit, brought actors to tears
Animal "Oscars" he won
But off he would run
And put a wrench in production gears

He caused such problems for his trainer
That dogs were hired as a restrainer
A dog at each door
Kept cat there, for sure
Dog use proved to be a "no brainer"

Orangey played the cat in Diary of Ann Frank
But his teammate skills totally "stank"
He was seen on TV
In the Batman series (1960's)
But actors wished he'd "walk the plank"*

*Just kidding.

NOTE: Orangey appeared in many films
and on TV shows. At the time, he was
the only cat to ever win two PATSY awards
for being the best animal star of the year.
The PATSY is the animal version of the
OSCAR. **Orangey** passed away in 1967
and is buried at Forest Lawn Memorial
Park in Los Angeles, CA.

CAN YOU "EAR" ME NOW?
PART 1

"Cat speak" involves many parts of me
Meow you hear, other things you see
If you pay attention and here I mention
That my ears tell you much, all agree

My long tail can stick up high
Tells you a lot, this I don't deny
But "ear" what I say, might make your day
Help you avoid a scratch cry

If my ears are up and facing you
With eyes like slits, I'm happy, not blue
Relaxed is my state, no need to wait
I might like to interact, too

BUT, if ears are high, erect, upright
And pupils are large, I just might
Be fearful, scared, feelin' some dread
And I might be ready to fight
SO GIVE ME SPACE!

ROOM 8

At Elysian Heights Elementary School
In the 1960's a cat did rule
Wandered into Room 8
Kids thought it was great
And the school became its "estate"

Room 8, the cat, was a male grey tabby
Who, unlike Orangey, was not crabby
He loved kids so
And each fall would show
And hang out with the kids in his "abby"*

Not sure why, but Room 8 he liked best
Kids named him that, knew they were blessed
When they left for summer
For him was a bummer
But each fall he returned with zest
*ABBY: HIS SACRED PLACE.

He became known in Southern Cal
And on kids' faces he brought a smile
Books about him were written
'Cause people were smitten
But none more than a child
In
Room 8

NOTE: Room 8 (the cat) became so famous
that a children's book was written about
him and he was featured in a major
magazine (1962). When he passed away
in 1968, he had his own obituary in the
Los Angeles Times. His paw prints are
immortalized in cement outside the
school. Room 8 now lies in rest at the
Pet Memorial in Calabasas, CA, where
he has his own gravestone.

CAN YOU "EAR" ME NOW?
PART 2

If ears look flat like airplane wings
I might scratch, you might scream
This do not ignore
Scared or angry for sure
And aggression's the emotion I bring
AGAIN, GIVE ME SPACE!

If you can see the backs of my ears
I'm ready to fight, feelin' some fear
Ears facing back say "back off, Jack"
My fear could result in your tears

So watch my ears and my tail, too
Both give wonderful signals to you
If my fur's out straight
Stop petting, don't wait
Because I am uptight, in a "stew"

NOW, HUMAN READER, YOU CAN
UNDERSTAND SOME
"CAT SPEECH"

TOWSER THE MOUSER

Towser the mouser mice did catch
Over 28,000 met their match
They thought they were slicker
But she was quicker
Holds the record for mice dispatched

Twas a long-haired tortoiseshell kitty
A special cat with colors so pretty
In Scottish town Crieff
She gave mice great grief
And was given the key to the city*

Over a long career of 24 years
She caused lots of mice great tears
Has a statue, for sure
That tourists can tour
If they find "mousers" quite dear

*I made that up; but, hey, it sounds like something
that should have happened.

Those pesky mice, they had no chance
And when Miss **Towser** started to prance
T'were in trouble so great
No way to escape
They'd already danced their last dance

NOTE: Yes, there is a bronze statue of **Towser** at the Glenturret Company in Crieff, Scotland. There is also a beverage named after her. She lived her entire life (nearly 24 years) at the Glenturret facility, and the Guinness Book of World Records' staff came up with the estimated number of mice she had "offed." **Towser** is one famous feline!

COATS OF MANY COLORS

Domestic house cats come in many colors. Here are some examples of coat colors, not breeds.

CALICO: Tricolor, any breed. Usually white with orange and black patches but could have other colors. They are almost exclusively female.

TABBY: Typically have an "M"-shaped mark on the forehead. Orange cats will always have a tabby pattern. Many cats are tabby.

TORTOISESHELL: Coat combines two colors, other than white. Colors could be closely mixed or in large patches. Some have a tabby pattern. They are almost all females.

TUXEDO: Coat is white plus one color. The most striking example is one with a black body and a white chest and paws – like a person dressed in a tuxedo (or an Emperor Penguin).

SOLID: Coat of one color only.

PICKLES: CATS AND WATER

Pickles, a kitten when I wrote this
Sees running water, thinks it is bliss
She'll sit in a sink
And then in a blink
Will shower with her human "sis"

If you fill up her water dish
She'll sit in it and her tail swish
If faucet drips
She just might sip
Or swat it if that's her wish

Tigers and jags do love to swim
Frolic in water, that's just them
But lions don't play
In water, they say
While some cougars really can swim

A mile or more. Can you relate?
They do this off Washington State
From mainland, you know
To islands they go
And Puget Sound is their "lake"

NOTE: Most cats are NOT fond of water. Some, like Pickles (a Siamese), will play in water in a variety of ways. While some Siamese cats can also swim, most domestic house cats will become totally annoyed if soaked with water.

The coats of a few domestic cat breeds repel water, but the rest just get soaking wet (which they do NOT like) when immersed.

As noted in the poem, some big cats take to water, while others do not.

THE EVOLUTION OF THE SOMEWHAT, PARTIALLY, SLIGHTLY AND A LITTLE BIT DOMESTICATED (MAYBE)

HOUSE CAT

We cats you never really do own
For in our minds, we sit on a throne
"Domestic" cat
Funny word, that
Know we could survive on our own

Let me just say, and I'll try to be nice
You wanted us because of those mice
You wanted them killed
And yes, we were thrilled
Moved in after checking things twice

We did this after checking our list
Free room and board? Hard to resist
You like us some places
And there still are traces
Of cat-headed gods in land that's
sun-kissed*

*Egypt

We're independent wherever we dwell
Do not always take instruction well
Free agents we remain
As we play the game
And might take off for a spell

Aloof but can be affectionate, yes
Serene and savage in our life's quest
Might exasperate you
Can be endearing, too
Much tolerance from you is best

Sailors* prob'ly first brought us here
But the details surely aren't clear
Columbus played a role
And the Mayflower, we're told
Now our numbers rise every year

We "semi-domesticated" pets now are
In our minds the best pets by far
In a third of your homes
Our kinfolk do roam
We think we're your biggest rock star

*Sailors, in the past, used cats on ships to
eliminate mice and protect their food supply.

A VERY SHORT
DOMESTIC CAT HISTORY

(WHAT WE THINK WE KNOW SO FAR)

What we now call the domestic house cat began its unique relationship with us over 10,000 years ago.

We do not know for certain where cats were first domesticated. Some think it was Egypt, others the Fertile Crescent, and still others think this occurred at multiple places around the same time.

Even if Egypt was not where the cat was first domesticated, it certainly played a major role in spreading cats throughout the world.

Cats could have traveled on Egyptian grain ships (where they were used to catch mice) and disembarked when the ship docked in another Mediterranean port. Columbus and other seafarers carried cats on their ships as "crew members" charged with catching mice. Some folks traveling on the Mayflower also brought cats with them.

Most animals were domesticated for milk, wool, or meat – but not the cat.

Some like to think we made a
conscious decision to domesticate the
cat. Others think the cat chose us
because of benefits like free room
and board and an ongoing supply of
mice to eat.

This idea may relate to the cat's unique
personality. Cats can be aloof, affectionate,
serene, savage, endearing and exasperating.
To me, they are like free agents on a pro
sports team. They might elect to stay with
you or they might bolt, only to return
at some later date.

An ancient Egyptian goddess had a cat head.

Humans and cats have had a mostly
symbiotic (both benefit) relationship
for thousands of years.

In U.S. homes, cats and dogs are the most
popular house pet. About one-third
of all U.S. homes have a cat.

THE CATIO

Cat services and products are a
BILLION DOLLAR INDUSTRY.

You can even buy a "catio" these
days for $260.00 or so.

This is an outdoor enclosure that can
be attached to your house. It can have
perches and scratching posts and easy
access for the lowly human to clean it.

The cat access to the catio may be
through a hole cut in your window
screen.

The catio lets the cat "sort of"
experience the outdoors without you
worrying about vehicle traffic, coyotes,
or pit bulls harming your pet.

SHORT CATALOG OF
ALPHA-CAT-ICAL WORDS

CATamount: a wild animal of the cat family.

CATs and dogs: quarrelsome.

CATastrophe: what happens when your cat knocks something over.

CATbird: a bird that can sound like a cat meowing.

CATbird seat: a position of power.

CAT burglar: a thief who enters a building by climbing.

CATclaw: a cat's claw.

CATerwauling: a cat's long, drawn out wailing cries; whining.

CAT-eyed: able to see in the dark.

CATfish: a type of fish that has whiskers.

CATfooted: sure-footed, noiseless, quiet, stealthy.

CATio: an outdoor enclosure/playhouse for a pet cat.

CATnap: a short nap.

CATnip: a plant with strongly scented leaves that cats like.

CATwalk: a narrow place to walk near the ceiling of a stage.

GUESS WHAT'S COMING NEXT

ABOUT THE AUTHOR

Wayne McDonald graduated from Stedman High School in Cumberland County, NC. He is also a graduate of the University of North Carolina, Chapel Hill, NC, where he obtained a Bachelor of Arts degree in Elementary Education and a Master of Education in Education Administration. While at UNC, he completed the U.S. Air Force ROTC program with distinction and was designated an Outstanding Graduate. He retired in the Denver, CO, area after an Air Force career that took him to Europe, Asia and multiple places in the U.S. He retired with the rank of Colonel. He is the recipient of multiple medals including the Legion of Merit. He has worked for Littleton Public Schools, Littleton, CO, and is currently serving as a Senior Volunteer, reading animal poems to elementary students. He also works for the First Tee Colorado Mountains and for the South Suburban Parks and Recreation District. Once a week or so, he reaffirms his status as a certified duffer at the South Suburban Golf Course in Centennial.

Website: www.pwmcdonald.com

ABOUT THE ILLUSTRATOR

 BJ McDonald, M.Ed. is a professional artist and educational specialist with over two decades of experience working with children. She channels both her artistic talents and her understanding of children's literature into her work. A self-taught artist, BJ has crafted her own unique style of vibrant, acrylic paintings over the years, drawing from her travels to paint compelling scenery. Her work, including her murals, can be found around the Denver Metro area. Outside of teaching and painting, BJ is a proud mother and a volunteer for the International Dyslexia Association-Rocky Mountain Branch.

www.bettyejean.com

 @bettyejeanart

IMPORTANT NOTE

My poems about real cats that lived or are living today are based on the various articles I found online.

My generic cat poems are based on articles I read, on my personal experience with cats as childhood pets, and on input from cat owners.

Now, the paintings: My research turned up info that, for example, tells you the cat is/was a black and white tabby. In some cases, the illustrator and the scribbler found nice colored pictures of the real cat. In other cases, we found different pictures of the same cat that showed the cat in different colored coats. AND, in other cases, we could not find a good colored picture of the cat. BOTTOM LINE: The paintings herein may not look exactly like the real cat.

With the Pickles painting, my wonderful Illustrator accurately painted the cat's facial expression but whimsically added coat colors not found on any house cat's coat. I think they call this "artistic expression." Pickles is my granddaughter's cat.

www.ingramcontent.com/pod-product-compliance
Lightning Source LLC
Chambersburg PA
CBHW041126120626
46547CB00019B/2867